THIS IS
A BOOK FOR
PEOPLE
WHO LOVE
MUSHROOMS

THIS IS
A BOOK FOR
PEOPLE
WHO LOVE
MUSHROOMS

MEG MADDEN

Illustrated by Hannah Bailey

RUNNING PRESS
PHILADELPHIA

Running Press
Hachette Book Group
1290 Avenue of the Americas, New York, NY 10104
www.runningpress.com
@Running_Press

Printed in China
First Edition: March 2023

Published by Running Press, an imprint of Perseus Books, LLC, a subsidiary of Hachette Book Group, Inc. The Running Press name and logo are trademarks of the Hachette Book Group.

The Hachette Speakers Bureau provides a wide range of authors for speaking events. To find out more, go to www.hachettespeakersbureau.com or call (866) 376-6591.

The publisher is not responsible for websites (or their content) that are not owned by the publisher.

Text by Meg Madden.

Print book cover and interior design by Jenna McBride.

Library of Congress Control Number: 2022942166

ISBNs: 978-0-7624-8136-1 (hardcover), 978-0-7624-8138-5 (ebook)

RRD-S

10 9 8 7 6 5 4 3 2 1

For Daisy, my Mushroom Muse

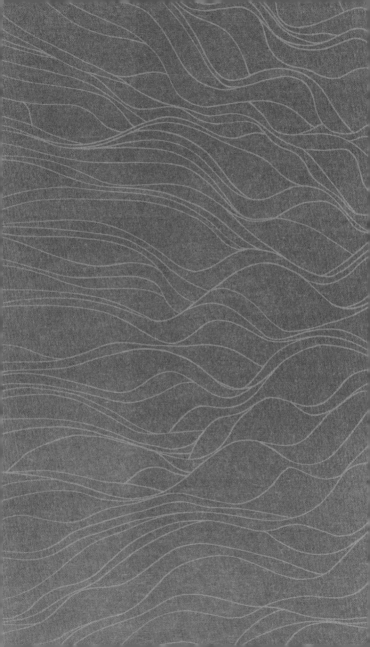

CONTENTS

What Is a Mushroom?

Ask just about anyone to draw a mushroom, and they'll likely sketch the classic toadstool: a tan- or red-domed cap—maybe with spots—a stem, and possibly some gills. These are the images of mushrooms many Americans are exposed to the most, whether through literature and popular culture or because these are the most common types found in US supermarkets and cuisine.

But in reality, mushrooms come in myriad shapes, textures, and sizes, as well as every color of the rainbow. Some are tiny bowls, cups, or spoons fit for faerie feasts. There are species that look like daisy-petaled flowers, discarded citrus peels, miniature birds' nests complete with eggs, and even wrinkled brains and spooky zombie fingers poking from the earth. Many have the appearance of ocean life—seashells, starfish, anemones, spiny urchins, squid tentacles, and fantastical branched corals—organisms that look like they would be more at home under the sea than growing from the forest floor. Some are so small they can hardly be seen with the naked eye, while some are so large they could barely fit in a wheelbarrow.

But what is a mushroom, exactly? Mushrooms are fruiting bodies; much like an apple is the reproductive structure of a tree, a mushroom is the visible reproductive structure of a fungus. Most of a fungus's mass exists largely out of view in the soil, under leaves and logs, and embedded in the substrate it is growing in. This hidden portion is made up of an extensive net of thread-like tissue called **mycelium**. Mycelium secretes enzymes for digestion and absorbs water and nutrients for the fungus. It also can connect plants and trees in a mutualistic network much like Mother Nature's internet. In a thriving environment, under ideal conditions, there can be an astounding seven to eight miles of mycelium in one cubic inch of soil.

One of the primary goals of living organisms is to reproduce and ensure the survival of their species. When it is time for fungi to do so, they form mushrooms, which in turn produce **spores** containing the fungal organism's genetic material. This process uses up a tremendous amount of energy and resources, so it must be timed wisely to take advantage of the moist conditions that most mushrooms require to reach reproductive maturity. This is why mushrooms are often found popping up in damp, shady forests and soggy lawns after a rainfall.

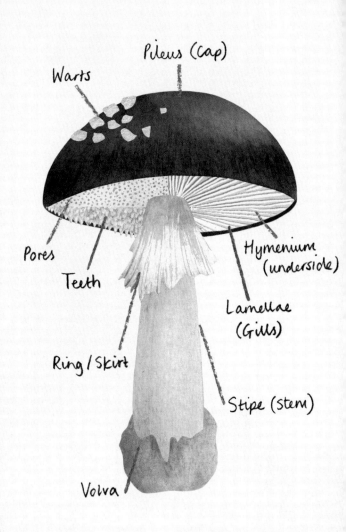

Warts

Pileus (Cap)

Pores

Teeth

Ring / Skirt

Hymenium (underside)

Lamellae (Gills)

Stipe (Stem)

Volva

Anatomy of a Mushroom

Not all mushrooms are shaped like the classic toadstool, but those that are have many of the same basic parts. For everyone from casual nature enthusiasts interested in mycology as a hobby to serious foragers, learning about these structures is key to becoming proficient at identifying wild mushrooms. Some edible mushrooms have toxic look-alikes, so careful observation and knowledge of each species' unique characteristics are especially important when foraging.

From our human perspective, the top of the mushroom is often the first part we observe, so it offers the first clues about a mushroom's identity. The cap is called a **pileus** in mycological terms. Think of a grilled portobello and you'll have a sense of exactly which part of the mushroom this is. A mushroom's cap serves as protection, structure, and support for the fertile surface found on the underside. Caps come in every color imaginable, from dull and subdued to shockingly bright. They can be smaller than the head of a pin or as large as an open umbrella, pointy like a witch's hat or concave like a dish. Their sheen ranges from dull and chalky to glossy as a sports car, and their endlessly diverse textures run the gamut from dry and leathery to gooey, slimy, warty, spiky, and even furry.

The more distinctive-looking mushrooms can be easily recognized solely by the features of their caps, but it is often necessary to study other parts of the mushroom as well. The underside of the cap is the next place to look. Called the **hymenium**, this is the fertile surface where spores are produced. Most people are familiar with gills, or **lamellae**, the ridges that radiate out from the stem like spokes on a wheel. The gills' color, spacing, and means of attachment to the stem can all be key to a mushroom's identity. The folds and ridges of the gills function to increase the surface area of the spore-producing hymenium. Other mushroom species have developed different means of maximizing this real estate. Some have evolved toothy projections, while others have developed long, spore-producing tubes that end in openings called **pores**.

A fungus's goal is not only to produce as many spores as possible but also to ensure they have the best chance of traveling the farthest. A mushroom's stem, or **stipe**, facilitates spore dispersal by elevating the fertile surface to an optimal height so spores can be distributed far and wide on air currents or carried by dining insects, hungry slugs and snails, passing animals, and even humans. Offering more clues about a mushroom's identity, stems can be as diverse looking as other mushroom parts. Like caps, they come in every color and texture imaginable. In stature, they can be long and slender like a hair or stout and stocky enough to dwarf the cap, giving them the appearance of a person wearing a tiny hat many sizes too small for their head.

Certain mushrooms have specialized structures that can further aid in their identification. One example is the **universal veil**, an egg-like structure found at or under the soil line that encases and protects the young mushroom when it is first developing. In species of *Amanita*, a portion of the universal veil remains at the base of the mushroom's stem as a bulb or cup-like sac called a **volva**. Immature stinkhorns are also enclosed in a universal veil. Some mushrooms have a **partial veil**—a thin, tissuey, cobwebby, or slimy membranous covering that protects the mushroom's developing gills. After the cap fully expands, this partial veil tissue is often left behind as a ring or pendant skirt-like structure on the stem and sometimes as raised warts or patches on the mushroom's cap.

Mushroom Classification and Names

Scientists categorize all living things into groups of similar organisms as a means of organization and to facilitate common communication about life on earth. Until the mid-nineteenth century there were two kingdoms of classification: animals and plants, and fungi were included with the latter. The rationale was that plants are rooted in place and produce their own food by means of photosynthesis. Animals, on the contrary, are free to move about but cannot make their own food. In the 1960s, as the life cycle of fungi became better understood—generally, that they can neither move nor make their own food—fungi finally got a kingdom of their own. Incidentally, fungi share a more recent common ancestor with animals than they do plants. That means that a morel is more closely related to you than to a daisy.

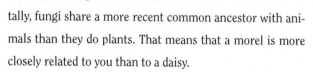

Fungi are further organized within this system into increasingly smaller groups based on shared characteristics.

Their common names, the ones with which we are most familiar, are often whimsical—elf cups, fairy fingers, earthstars—or describe their appearance—hedgehog, coral, peanut butter cups. As descriptive as they are, these colloquial names can vary from region to region and country to country, leading to potential confusion. This is why the scientists who study fungi, known as mycologists, give each one an official genus and species name—usually with roots in Latin and Greek—so that everyone in the world, no matter their language, can accurately recognize them.

In reference materials, fungi are often listed by a common name first, followed by the genus and species names in italics. Until modern genetics, fungi were filed into these classifications based on their morphology, or physical appearance. The development of DNA sequencing has since turned this system on its head, and there has been a mass renaming of species and shuffling of fungi from one group to another ever since. Because mycologists are continually in the process of untangling fungal DNA, outdated genus and species names are common in older field guides and even on the internet.

Ecological Roles of Fungi

Fungi are everywhere—in our lawns and forests, in and on our bodies, and even lurking in that forgotten Tupperware container in the back of the fridge. While some fungi are harmful, the vast majority are beneficial to their environments and serve important ecological roles.

Some fungi act as parasites, infecting their hosts and sickening or even killing them. Common human ailments such as ringworm and athlete's foot are caused by fungi. Pathogenic fungi like rusts and mildews regularly cause costly damage to important agricultural crops. Chestnut blight, *Cryphonectria parasitica*, was inadvertently introduced to North America from Southeast Asia at the turn of the twentieth century and in a few short decades wiped out billions of chestnut trees in the United States, nearly causing their extinction. Fungi even attack other fungi. *Hypomyces lactifluorum* parasitizes species of *Lactarius* and *Russula*, transforming them into the choice edible known as the lobster mushroom.

Hands down, though, the fungal parasites that infect insects have to be among the most bizarre. These fungi keep their insect hosts alive but take complete control of their actions, using them as zombie minions to spread their spores for them.

A second group of fungi are the decomposers known as **saprobes**. Humans have a primal aversion to rotting things, developed to help us avoid eating spoiled food that could cause illness. But decay is an essential part of an ecosystem's natural cycle and decomposers are nature's recycling crew. They feed on dead organic matter, breaking it down  into nutrients that can then be used by other organisms, and life begins anew. As the only multicellular organisms capable of breaking down lignin, the toughest parts of wood and leaves, fungi act as nature's cleanup crew. Without them, every tree that has ever died would still be lying about in huge piles like enormous pick-up sticks, and the earth would be buried under an epic leaf pile.

The third group of fungi enter into mutualistic relationships, called **mycorrhiza**, with plants, including food crops and the trees in our forests. In fact, about 90 percent of land plants rely on partnerships with mycorrhizal fungi. Underground microscopic fungal filaments, called **hyphae**, connect with plant rootlets, forming a symbiotic bond. The plant, then tapped into the massive mycelial network of the fungus, has much greater access to nutrients and water. As part of this ancient bartering system, the fungus receives sugars that the plant produces during photosynthesis, a food the fungus is incapable of making itself. In healthy forests, trees connected via this network, sometimes called the "wood wide web," can even share water and nutrients with each other. The trees can detect stress in their neighbors and send extra resources their way via the mycelial network to help them through tough times such as periods of drought. The largest and most deeply rooted of these trees are the mother trees. These woodland giants have the capability of linking with hundreds of other trees through their vast, radiating mycelial connections. They share with younger saplings that may otherwise struggle for resources in their highly competitive forest environment. Interestingly, studies have shown that mother trees favor their own seedlings over the seedlings of other trees.

The Fungus Among Us

I t is thought that only about 5 percent of the earth's fungal species are known to humans. Thanks to modern science, intrepid mycologists, and even community scientists, that number is increasing all the time. Compared with what we know about plants and animals, our knowledge of fungi is limited. This may be in part because the bulk of a fungus's mass is hidden from view—a kind of "out of sight, out of mind" situation. For the most part these organisms tend to live under the radar, making themselves visible primarily when it's time to make more fungi. Whether we're conscious of it or not, though, fungi impact our daily lives in both small and profound ways—we are as inextricably intertwined with them as the mycelial web itself.

In their most obvious role, fungi provide us with sustenance in the form of mushrooms. They are more than just delicious; they are high in fiber and a good source of protein, antioxidants, vitamins, and minerals while low in calories, carbs, and fat. Fungi are used extensively in the production of many widely consumed food products—you can thank yeasts and molds, both types of fungi, for wine, beer, coffee, bread, cheese, and even chocolate. Mycoprotein-based meat substitutes are gaining in popularity for ethical  and health reasons and because fungiculture has less of an impact on the environment and is less costly than traditional livestock farming. In a less obvious sense, fungi also play an integral role in our food system by building soil health and as mycorrhizal partners for agricultural crop plants.

Just as they can cause illness, fungi are the source for many important pharmaceuticals. Most of the top prescription drugs in the United States are synthesized from plants and fungi. These include drugs used to treat cancer and high cholesterol, as well as antibiotics. The first antibiotic to be isolated from a fungus was penicillin, discovered by Scottish physician Alexander Fleming in 1928. Penicillin, still used today, was incredibly difficult to manufacture at first but was spurred into mass production by the tremendous loss of life due to bacterial infections during World War II. The headline of an ad printed in a 1944 issue of *Life* magazine declared, "Thanks to PENICILLIN...he will come home!"

In Eastern cultures, mushrooms have been used for centuries to boost the immune and nervous systems, to treat countless ailments such as inflammatory diseases and cancer, and to support mental health and overall vigor and vitality. Traditional medicinal mushrooms such as turkey tail, lion's mane, reishi, chaga, and *Cordyceps* are quickly becoming more mainstream in the West, too. These "functional" mushrooms, mushrooms that have health benefits beyond their nutritional value, are now widely available as supplements. And they're not just embraced by the alternative health crowd—universities and big pharmaceutical companies are spearheading cutting-edge clinical trials to test and hone their efficacy as treatment for many of modern society's toughest health issues.

Entheogens, naturally occurring psychoactive substances, have been used in the spiritual ceremonies of Indigenous peoples for thousands of years. In the United States in the mid-1950s, psilocybin—a psychoactive substance found in most species of the genus *Psilocybe*—was being studied for its therapeutic benefits as an aid to psychotherapy treatment for certain mental health disorders. This early research, spearheaded by a group of psychology professors, even had the backing of one of America's most prestigious universities. These psychoactive mushrooms, dubbed "magic mushrooms" or "'shrooms," went on to gain public notoriety as a recreational drug during the 1960s when their mind-expanding properties became an integral part of the free-thinking hippie movement. In the early 1970s, the US government launched the war on drugs as backlash against America's youth counterculture, who had been rocking the boat with their political views, protests against the Vietnam War, unconventional alternative lifestyle, and use of psychedelic drugs to "turn on, tune in, and drop out." The unfortunate result was that in 1970 psilocybin was listed as Schedule I under the Controlled Substances Act, lumped in with heroin and other highly addictive drugs deemed to have no currently accepted medical use. Consequently, research into the clinical benefits of psychedelics came to a screeching halt, but attitudes about the substance have evolved with time. Fast-forward several decades and psilocybin is now once again the subject of cutting-edge medical research, showing great promise for a multitude of applications such as treating individuals with PTSD, severe depression, and substance use disorder, and alleviation of end-of-life distress for the terminally ill.

The Future Is Fungi

I n response to the climate crisis, scientists are increasingly interested in the roles that fungi can play to help meet climate change goals now and far into the future. Humans are consuming more resources than the planet can sustainably produce and creating more waste than we can process in an environmentally responsible manner, which is taking a toll on the world. Industries that contribute significantly to consumption, the waste stream, and pollution are turning to applied mycology—ways that fungi can be used as affordable, sustainable, eco-friendly, low-environmental-impact solutions to some of these challenges.

For example, the construction industry is looking into the viability of mycelium-based green building materials. Fungal mycelium grows quickly and can be easily formed into bricks, insulation, and other components, using minimal resources and therefore having a greatly reduced environmental footprint. Once cured, mycelium-based materials are incredibly strong and durable, and are highly resistant to moisture, mold, and fire. Nontoxic and completely biodegradable, instead of becoming landfill at the end of their use, they can be composted or even used as a substrate for growing food.

Visionaries in the world of clothing and textiles, an industry with one of the biggest negative environmental impacts, are turning to mushroom pigments for eco-friendly dyes to replace highly toxic chemicals, and mycelium-based biofabrics as an alternative to traditional cloth such as cotton, which uses a tremendous amount of water, herbicides, and pesticides to produce. Fungi-based textiles are soft, durable, breathable, and naturally antimicrobial. This may seem like futuristic science fiction, but fungi fashion is already hitting the runways—and becoming more widely available to the general public—in the form of clothing made from mycelium, and shoes, jackets, and purses made from vegan mushroom leather.

There is great potential for fungi to play a critical role in cleaning up waste, pollutants, and environmental disasters. Mycoremediation—which literally means "fungus restoring balance"—is a form of biological remediation that uses living organisms to remove contaminants from soil and freshwater and marine environments. Certain fungi can survive in extreme conditions where most organisms cannot, making them ideal for use in isolating and breaking down agricultural and industrial pollutants, oil spills, and even radiation. Some fungi are able to remove heavy metals from the environment by bioaccumulating them in their tissues. There are even mushrooms that can digest plastic. For example, *Pestalotiopsis microspora* can survive solely on polystyrene as its food source. Plastic can take hundreds of years to decompose on its own, but the mycelium of *P. microspora* begins to break it down into organic matter in a few short weeks and can digest it completely within a few months' time. Ideally, this biotechnology could be utilized in both small-scale applications such as home recycling kits, which would put plastic reduction into the hands of individuals; and because it can thrive in conditions where there is no light or air, it is a perfect candidate for large-scale municipal projects such as cleaning up landfills. Even the common edible oyster mushroom (*Pleurotus ostreatus*) can consume plastic. If ongoing research proves that they are safe to eat once they have done their job, these humble mushrooms could potentially perform the dual duty of reducing plastic waste while helping to alleviate famine and food insecurity.

Foraging for Mushrooms

A merican mycologist and author David Arora wrote, "We are creatures of the earth whose most ancient heritage…is foraging for food in the forest." Indeed, gathering has been an important part of our survival since prehistoric times. Before agriculture and industry, early humans relied on wild plants and mushrooms for both food and medicine. In 1991 the mummified remains of a Copper Age man more than five thousand years old were found partially embedded in a glacier between Italy and Austria. Named Ötzi after the mountains in which he was discovered, he was carrying two species of polypore mushroom: birch polypore (*Fomitopsis betulina*), likely used for medicine, and tinder conk (*Fomes fomentarius*), as part of a fire-starting kit.

Foraging is a lucrative form of income in many parts of the world. Some mushrooms such as morels, chanterelles, and porcini are difficult or impossible to cultivate commercially, so they must be hand-gathered from the wild. When fresh local mushrooms are available, some chefs will design entire menus around what is in season. Truffle hunting is alive and well in France and Italy, where the trade of these highly sought-after mushrooms is big business. Specially bred and highly trained dogs such as the Lagotto Romagnolo have replaced pigs— which would sometimes eat the truffles they found—to sniff out the luxuriously fragrant underground treasures. European truffles are, ounce for ounce, the most expensive food in the world, fetching thousands of dollars per pound. A two-pound (.9kg) white truffle sold for a record $330,000 in 2010.

Foraging can be a rewarding hobby. Not only is it a source of free gourmet food, it's a great way to get outside and connect with nature. Both for success and for safety, foragers must have a working knowledge of specific ecosystems and the trees that grow in them as well as a keen awareness of weather patterns and seasons. Learning to identify mushrooms with 100 percent certainty is a must, as there are sometimes only subtle differences between delicious edibles and toxic look-alikes. It is highly advisable for novice foragers to confirm ID with a mycologist or professional forager because a misidentification could have an unfortunate diner camping out in the bathroom with a severe case of gastrointestinal distress or worse. For example, the only treatment for ingesting the deadly toxic destroying angel (*Amanita bisporigera*) is an emergency liver transplant. The forager's credo, and a good rule to *literally* live by, is "when in doubt, throw it out"—or, better, leave it where you found it. And even mushrooms that are widely consumed can be indigestible to some people. When eating a new species for the first time, always try a small amount to be sure it doesn't upset your stomach before enjoying a whole meal of it.

In many parts of Europe, foraging is a national pastime, with knowledge passed down from generation to generation. French pharmacists are trained to identify common mushrooms and will look over a forager's basket, free of charge, to weed out any toxic species. In the United States, where foraging is not part of the culture in the same way, foraging and eating wild mushrooms can be a scary prospect. This fear of mushrooms even has a name—mycophobia. Foraging in the States is becoming increasingly popular, and with proper education and training even the beginner forager can fairly easily identify some edible varieties. Mushroom hunting is often a slippery slope; once they've had a taste, so to speak, many folks find themselves wanting to learn more. Though there is a wealth of information in books and on the internet, for those who wish to move beyond the basics, taking foraging classes or joining a local mushroom club is highly advised. Nothing can take the place of hands-on learning with an expert.

A seasoned forager has spent a great deal of time and energy accumulating vast knowledge of mushrooms and their habits. They have likely walked many miles, suffered a thousand insect bites, tangled with poisonous plants, and persevered through every kind of weather to find the most productive mushroom spots. In other words, don't expect them to give up all their secrets—at least not right away. American nature poet Mary Oliver may have best summed up the heart of a mushroom hunter: "Ordinarily I go into the woods alone, not with a single friend....If you have ever gone into the woods with me, I must love you very much."

MUSHROOM
PROFILES

BIRD'S NEST FUNGUS

Crucibulum laeve

It is always a treat to find these adorable little mushrooms, which are often overlooked because of their diminutive size. Resembling tiny nests complete with itty-bitty eggs, it's not hard to see how this mushroom earned its common name, bird's nest fungus.

Bird's nest fungi have a very unusual and effective reproductive adaptation. The eggs, actually tiny spore-containing capsules called **peridioles**, are tethered to the inside of the nest-like cup by means of sticky strings. The nest acts as a splash cup: when raindrops land inside, they launch the peridioles into the air and up to a meter or more away. The sticky strings adhere to the surfaces on which they land, and if conditions are favorable, the peridioles will split to release spores and continue the fungus's life cycle.

Bird's nest fungi are fairly common in urban settings such as parks, playgrounds, and gardens, where they live happily on bark mulch and decaying matter under bushes and in other cool, shady, moist nooks. A thriving colony can contain hundreds, if not thousands, of nests. Sometimes homeowners are concerned that mushrooms in their lawn, garden—or even flower pots—are a worrisome sign, but they are harmless and can actually be an indicator of healthy soil. Bird's nest mushrooms may be small, but they are mighty—a real gardener's friend—performing the big, important job of decomposing wood and garden debris into nutrients that can be used by nearby plants.

HABITAT & ECOLOGY: Saprobic on decaying wood, particularly small twigs, and even dung, in moist, shady wooded areas. Commonly found in yards and parks on bark mulch, or even discarded timber and plywood. Colonies of hundreds of fruiting bodies can be so dense that individual nests become distorted from overcrowding.

DISTRIBUTION: Widely distributed.

SEASON: Spring through fall, and over winter in milder areas.

PHYSICAL DESCRIPTION: Nests are up to ⅓" (1 cm) high and wide, at first drum shaped and covered by a velvety, dull, yellow-orange membrane. As the mushroom expands and matures into a bowl shape, the membrane ruptures to reveal five to eight whitish-tan 1.5 mm eggs tethered by thin, sticky strings. Mature nests range in color from dull yellow-orange to brown and are smooth or velvety outside and shiny and smooth on the inner surface.

BLACK TRUMPET

Craterellus fallax and *C. cornucopioides*

Black trumpets, also known as horn of plenty, *trompette de la mort* (France), and *trombetta dei morti* (Italy), are one of the world's most sought-after culinary mushrooms. They smell amazing—earthy, smoky, floral, and a little sweet, with a delectable flavor to match. They do not have any toxic look-alikes, making them a great choice for beginning foragers.

Finding them is the tricky part. Sometimes called the "black holes of the forest," it's not that they are uncommon—it's that they are hard to spot. They look like little black funnels sticking out of the forest floor, and their dark color and particular shape blends in perfectly with the shadowy leaf-littered ground of their preferred habitat. The good news is, if you manage to spot one, you are likely to find more, as they tend to grow in clusters and can blanket large areas by the hundreds.

Black trumpets, also referred to as black chanterelles, and other members of the genus *Craterellus* are commonly lumped in with the true chanterelles of the genus *Cantharellus*. Though thinner fleshed than true chanterelles, they are all delicious edibles and include such species as the flame chanterelle (*C. ignicolor*), and the yellowfoot chanterelle (*C. tubaeformis*).

HABITAT & ECOLOGY: Mycorrhizal with oaks and beech in mixed deciduous forests, sometimes growing in mossy areas.

DISTRIBUTION: *C. fallax* widely distributed east of the Rocky Mountains; *C. cornucopioides* common on the West Coast from the Santa Cruz Mountains northward.

SEASON: *C. fallax* spring through fall, *C. cornucopioides* winter through spring.

PHYSICAL DESCRIPTION: Completely hollow at all stages, black trumpets have dry, thin, brittle flesh. Young fruiting bodies are narrow tubes that become deeply trumpet- or vase-shaped at maturity. The upper outrolled margins often become heavily frilled, ruffled, and cracked with age. The inner surface is dark brown to black, while the outer, finely wrinkled spore-bearing surface is salmon- to ochre-colored for *C. fallax* and powdery gray for *C. cornucopioides.* Mature specimens are commonly up to 2" (5 cm) wide and 4" (10 cm) tall but can occasionally grow to twice that size.

BONNET

Mycena Species

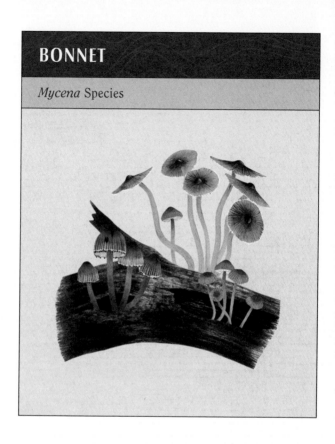

Though small in stature, bonnet mushrooms, representing about five hundred species worldwide, are quite beautiful. Sporting classic umbrella-shaped caps, gorgeous gills, and elegantly long, wiry stems, they often fruit in rather pictur-esque little groupings worthy of the pages of fairytales.

Although many bonnet species are muted tones of gray, tan, brown, and white, some are very colorful, and some species are even bioluminescent. Fresh specimens of the blue-foot bonnet (*Mycena amicta*) of the West Coast and the blue mycena (*M. subcaerulea*) of the eastern United States are both a lovely shade of rarely seen-in-nature sky blue. As they age, their vibrant color fades to tan and gray, making it difficult to distinguish them from their bland-colored cousins. Bleeding fairy helmets (*M. haematopus*), with caps and gills a charming shade of rosy pink, have deeper-red stems and "bleed" brilliant blood-red liquid when damaged. With their striking red-margined gills, Orange mycena mushrooms (*M. leaiana*) emerge from decaying logs in dense clusters, lending pops of brilliant color to the shadier nooks of the forest.

HABITAT & ECOLOGY: Saprobic on decaying organic matter, particularly sticks, branches, and logs, but sometimes on moist leaves or needle duff. Occasionally solitary but often fruiting in dense clusters of dozens or more mushrooms.

DISTRIBUTION: blue-foot bonnet, *Mycena amicta*—western United States; blue mycena, *M. subcaurulea*—eastern United States; bleeding fairy helmet, *M. haematopus*—widespread; orange mycena, *M. leaiana*—eastern United States.

SEASON: Year-round depending on the location and species.

PHYSICAL DESCRIPTION: Caps up to 2" (5 cm) across and oval, conical, or nearly cylindrical when young. Becoming broadly bell shaped or convex at maturity, sometimes with a central bump and striations around the edge. Color varies by species. Closely spaced gills are attached to the ½" to 3" (1 cm–8 cm) long thin, hollow, stringy-textured stem. Spore print white.

CATERPILLAR CLUB FUNGUS

Cordyceps militaris

While many fungi derive their nutrients from breaking down dead organic matter, some are parasitic. The strangest and most macabre of these are entomopathogenic, utilizing insects as their hosts. The caterpillar club fungus infects moth and butterfly pupae and larvae that are buried in well-rotted wood or soil. The fungus grows tissue throughout the insect, consuming and replacing its organs, mummifying it from the inside out. Once the fungus has gained enough mass, it forms a fruiting body that erupts out of the insect and emerges from the soil to produce mature spores and start the process all over again.

Since mushrooms can't move around on their own, some species of entomopathogenic fungi have developed an ingenious reproductive adaptation that tricks certain insects into giving them a free ride. They not only infect their host insect; they keep it alive and control its behavior, ensuring maximum spore dispersal over the largest possible area. *Massospora cicadina* turns cicadas into zombies, willing them to mate with reckless abandon despite the fact that their abdomen, along with their reproductive organs, has been replaced by fungal tissue. Species of the genus *Ophiocordyceps* play mind-control games with ants, causing them to climb onto nearby plants at just the right height to take advantage of optimal moisture and wind currents. After an infected ant has clamped its jaws firmly into a leaf, the fungus sends a fruiting body through its head, where it will mature and rain down spores onto the ant colony below.

Who needs to watch sci-fi movies when you can read about these truly bizarre fungal organisms instead?

HABITAT & ECOLOGY: Parasitic on pupae and larvae of moths and butterflies, found primarily in moist, mossy woodland. Other species of entomopathic fungi target ants, cicadas, and even spiders.

DISTRIBUTION: *Cordyceps militaris*—eastern North America, very rare in the Pacific Northwest. Many other species of entomopathic fungi are widespread.

SEASON: Summer and fall.

PHYSICAL DESCRIPTION: Bright orange, slender, club-shaped fruiting bodies are up to 2" (5 cm) long by up to ¼" (6 mm) in diameter. The surface is covered in raised spore-producing structures, giving it a subtle pebbled texture. Careful excavation of the soil around the fruiting body will reveal the buried pupae or larvae attached to its base.

CHANTERELLE

Cantharellus Species

Chanterelles are one of the most widely sought-after edible mushrooms, among the top culinary varieties along with morels and truffles. Classic golden chanterelles are also known as *girolle* in France, the country first responsible for bringing them to light as a delicacy. Coveted by chefs and foragers alike, they have a light, peppery taste and an intoxicating scent reminiscent of apricots. They're delicious simply sautéed in a little butter or added to uncomplicated cream-based sauces and soups, where their exquisite flavor can be appreciated. Chanterelles command a high price because of their gourmet status and because they require unique growing conditions, including a complex symbiosis with certain trees, making them nearly impossible to cultivate commercially.

The term "chanterelle" is used for several different mushrooms. In the United States golden chanterelles are not actually a single species but a group of genetically similar species that share common physical characteristics. Because they are difficult to tell apart, they are currently known collectively as the *Cantharellus cibarius* group.

Many other chanterelle varieties can be found growing in one form or another across most of the country. The cinnabar, or red, chanterelle (*C. cinnabarinus*) found in the East is much smaller than a golden chanterelle, but its brilliant salmon pink to tangerine orange color is striking on the plate. West of the Rocky Mountains, foragers can find such species as the California golden chanterelle (*C. californicus*), the Pacific golden chanterelle (*C. formosus*), and the white chanterelle (*C. subalbidus*).

HABITAT & ECOLOGY: Fruiting in small to very large groups, sometimes in arcs or rings around trees among fallen leaves and forest duff. Easy to spot because of their brilliant coloring. Mycorrhizal with various species of tree, predominantly conifers in the West and a variety of hardwoods and conifers in the East.

DISTRIBUTION: Widely distributed.

SEASON: Summer in the eastern United States, fall and early winter in the West.

PHYSICAL DESCRIPTION: These thick, meaty, vase-shaped mushrooms are classically bright golden egg-yolk yellow, while some species have white gills and stem or are creamy white overall. *C. cinnabarinus* is bright pinkish-orange. Medium-large 2" to 8" (3 cm–20 cm) wide caps are flat, shallowly depressed, or concave on top, often with ruffled edges. Chanterelles have "false" gills—blunt-edged forked folds and wrinkles that run well down the thick, blocky 2" to 5" (5 cm–12 cm) stem. Spore print white, creamy, yellow, pink, or salmon depending on the species.

CHICKEN OF THE WOODS

Laetiporus Species

Also known as sulphur shelf, chicken of the woods is one of a handful of easily distinguishable edible wild mushrooms that, armed with the proper knowledge, even the casual forager can be confident about identifying. Not to be confused with hen of the woods, another large, edible species in more muted shades of brown, the intense bright orange and yellow coloring of chicken of the woods, combined with their substantial size, makes them easy to spot. The individual fan-shaped mushrooms are large—up to a foot (30 cm) across—and often grow in huge, overlapping clusters. A single log or stump can yield enough mushrooms to fill a wheelbarrow.

Chicken of the woods gets its common name not from its appearance but from its taste and consistency. When cooked, its meaty, stringy texture makes a very convincing substitute for chicken. A small percentage of people experience gastrointestinal upset from consuming chicken of the woods, though, so as with all wild edible mushrooms, eat only a small portion the first time to be sure it is tolerated.

Because of their orange color and tendency to fruit in large clusters on wood, toxic jack o' lantern mushrooms (*Omphalotus* sp.) can, at first glance, be mistaken for chicken of the woods. A look at the underside will clear up any confusion. Jack o' lantern mushrooms have gills and well-defined stems, whereas chicken of the woods are polypores, meaning that the underside is covered in tiny pores instead of gills, and they lack a distinctive stem.

HABITAT & ECOLOGY: Lightly parasitic to saprobic on various types of wood depending on the species. Fruiting singly or in medium to large groups of densely overlapping clusters on logs, stumps, or live trees. Some species grow in rosettes at the bases of trees or on buried roots, appearing to grow from the soil.

DISTRIBUTION: *L. cincinnatus* and *L. sulphureus*—east of the Great Plains; *L. conifericola*—west of the Rocky Mountains; *L. gilbertsonii*—West Coast; *L. huroniensis*—upper Midwest and eastern United States.

SEASON: Summer and fall, through early winter in mild climates.

PHYSICAL DESCRIPTION: Thick and meaty shelf-like brackets are bright orange with a yellow edge where the mushrooms are actively growing. The upper surfaces display concentric bands of orange and yellow, or cream and peachy orange depending on the species. Lumpy and blob-like when young, individual fruiting bodies, up to 12" (30 cm) across, become fan shaped with lobed, wavy margins. The yellow to white undersurface is moist and spongy when young and covered in tiny pores. Older specimens become dry and chalky. Spore print white.

CONIFER-CONE CAP

Baeospora myosura

Beyond the typical places mushrooms reside—damp soil, decaying wood, rotting organic matter—some are very particular about where they grow. Fruiting on blades of grass, acorn caps, nuts, bones, animal dung, and even on the surfaces of other mushrooms, some species are easily identifiable by the fun, unusual, and peculiar places they call home.

The conifer-cone cap is one of a small handful of whimsical mushrooms that lives on fallen pine cones. These tiny, charming mushrooms can grow in great numbers, poking out from the spaces between the scales of the cones of several species of conifer across North America. In the eastern United States, they can often be found happily fruiting away on the cones of white pine, while they prefer Douglas fir and Sitka spruce cones west of the Rocky Mountains.

There is an advantage to being such a specialist. Generalist species that are not picky about what they grow on must vie against other generalist competitors for food, water, and other necessities for their survival. By evolving to complete their life cycle on cones, the conifer-cone cap has eliminated this factor, allowing it to spend less energy vying for resources and more energy making more adorable little pine-cone-dwelling mushrooms.

HABITAT & ECOLOGY: Saprobic on the cones of conifers, especially white pine, fir, and spruce. Occasionally fruiting alone but more often found sprouting by the dozens from a single cone.

DISTRIBUTION: Widely distributed.

SEASON: Fall in the eastern United States, fall and winter in warmer areas.

PHYSICAL DESCRIPTION: Cap ⅓" to ½" (1 cm–3 cm) across, convex at first and flattening out with age, tan in the center, fading to buff at the edges as it matures. The light-colored gills are closely spaced and attached to the stem. The long, thin stem, up to 2" (5 cm) in length, has conspicuous white thread-like hairs at the base where it attaches to its substrate. Spore print white.

CORAL FUNGUS

Various Species

Coral fungi are a colorful, visually stunning group of mushrooms, and as their name suggests, they look like they belong under the sea. Species of coral fungi, with their similar structures, might seem related, but they actually belong to a number of different genera that evolved separately from one another. This phenomenon, called convergent evolution, is a biological process whereby distantly related organisms develop similar physical or useful traits. Other examples of convergent evolution are flight in bats and birds, and the fins of fish and dolphins.

Coral fungi's fantastical forms aren't just for looks. Because they produce spores over their entire exterior, their many upright branches serve the same purpose as gills—to increase their fertile surface area. Some corals have profuse forked branches that originate from the same fleshy base, sort of like cauliflower having a wild hair day. From fingertip-sized specimens to whoppers weighing several pounds, they are commonly found in subdued shades of white, tan, and beige, but they also come in a variety of eye-popping hues. The red corals *Ramaria stuntzii* and *R. araiospora* range in color from scarlet to neon pink. Yellow tipped coral (*R. formosa*) has glowing peachy-salmon branches tipped in sunny yellow, young green tipped coral (*R. apiculata*) sports lime green highlights over tan, and violet coral (*Clavaria*) is an intense neon purple with magenta undertones.

Other varieties, often referred to as club or spindle fungi, form slender, unbranched finger-shaped fruiting bodies that arise singly or in tightly packed clusters. Groups of golden spindles (*Clavulinopsis fusiformis*) and orange spindle coral (*C. aurantiocinnabarina*) are like miniature campfires complete with licking flames, purple squid coral (*Alloclavaria purpurea*) looks like a miniature kraken waving its tentacles from the forest floor, and the eerie *Clavaria fragilis*, commonly known as fairy fingers or white worm coral, is aptly named for its clusters of long, ghostly appendages.

Some varieties of coral mushrooms are edible, but identification down to species can be extremely difficult. While most are not severely toxic, they can cause gastrointestinal upset, and their flavors range from bland to bitter and even burning. The edible crown-tipped coral (*Artomyces pyxidatus*) is a bit easier to identify. It fruits in airy clusters of delicate white to buff upright branches that end in tiny crown-shaped appendages. It always grows directly from wood, unlike similarly branched *Ramaria* species that grow from soil. While the crown-tipped coral is too insubstantial for an entire meal, it is a beautiful garnish for soups and can be added to seafood dishes to enhance their ocean aesthetic.

HABITAT & ECOLOGY: Solitary, in scattered groups, or fruiting in large troops under both hardwoods and conifers. Some species are thought to be mycorrhizal; others are saprobic on leaf litter, needle duff, and buried woody debris; while some grow from dead wood such as logs.

DISTRIBUTION: Widely distributed.

SEASON: Spring through fall in much of the United States, and fall into winter in temperate zones such as the Redwood Coast of California.

PHYSICAL DESCRIPTION: Color highly variable. Size ranges ¾" to 8" (2–15 cm) tall by ¾" to 10" (2–25 cm) across. The forked, multibranched stems of coral fungi arise from a common base, which can be slender to very stocky, and the very brittle branches range in stature from light and airy to thickly dense. Club fungi grow singly or in groups of multiple long, slender, fragile fruiting bodies, which can occasionally be twisted or grooved longitudinally.

EYELASH CUP

Scutellinia scutellata

The world of fungi includes a truly eccentric cast of characters. The wonderfully weird eyelash cup, or Molly eyewinker, is a prime example. Have you ever felt like you're being watched while walking alone through the forest? If so, there might have been eyelash cup fungi spying on you from a nearby log. Stunningly beautiful, their pretty deep orange to scarlet disc-shape fruiting bodies are enough reason to seek out these extremely tiny mushrooms. However, they are best known for their whimsically amusing outer ring of dark hairs that resemble long, thick eyelashes.

Usually about the size of a peppercorn and rarely reaching the size of a fingertip, their itty-bitty stature can make them quite challenging to spot. Their propensity to hide out in low, damp places, and in the nooks and crannies of rotting stumps and logs can make it even trickier to find them, but the hunt, even on hands and knees, is well worth the joy of gazing into their funky, fringed fungi eyes.

Sometimes found growing alongside, the lighter-colored orange eyelash cup (*Scutellinia erinaceus*) is so small as to be dwarfed by even the Molly eye winker. Barely visible to the naked eye, a hand lens is necessary to see their minute eyelashes. What they lack in size they make up for in numbers, as this species can be extremely prolific, fruiting by the thousands to densely fill a crack in the bark of a branch, or the entire surface of a log.

HABITAT & ECOLOGY: Saprobic on damp soil rich in organic matter or shady nooks and crannies of soggy logs and branches that no longer have any bark. Occasionally solitary but more often fruiting in groups.

DISTRIBUTION: Widely distributed.

SEASON: Spring through fall.

PHYSICAL DESCRIPTION: Young fruiting bodies, spherical at first and densely hairy, open up into shallow dish-shaped cups which are up to ½" (13 mm) at maturity. The inner fertile surface is bright to dark orange; the outer sterile surface is duller orange to brownish and covered in rows of fine, stiff, dark hairs that become thicker and longer around the outer margin of the cup. This species has no stem, the cup being attached directly to its substrate. Spore print white.

FLY AGARIC

Amanita muscaria

Amanita is a large genus encompassing approximately 600 species, with more than 120 found in the United States alone. Although some are safe to eat, the genus also contains some of the deadliest mushrooms on the planet. The death cap (*A. phalloides*) and the destroying angels (*A. bisporigera*

and *A. ocreata*), all fatally toxic, can be easily confused with very similar-looking edible mushrooms, so consumption of *Amanitas* is not generally recommended, especially for novice foragers.

Thanks to video games, emojis, and classic toadstool imagery generously sprinkled throughout popular culture, the red-and-white-spotted fly agaric is easily the most iconic mushroom in the world. There is even speculation that it has inspired many Christmas traditions, including the color scheme of Santa Claus's customary garb.

Amanita muscaria mushrooms are poisonous, containing several toxins and the psychoactive compound muscimol. It is thought that some cultures have used their hallucinogenic properties to induce visions during religious rituals. Eating them, however, is not recommended, as they can cause a host of unpleasant side effects such as nausea, drowsiness, agitation, low blood pressure, salivation, and headaches. Though fatalities are uncommon, in cases of extreme poisoning, delirium, seizures, and coma can occur. Despite their toxicity, they are consumed as a culinary mushroom in many parts of the world after the water-soluble toxins are removed through a methodical, multistep boiling process.

The red-and-white North American variety is considered a subspecies of the mushrooms found in Europe. Several other subspecies of *A. muscaria*—all with distinctive coloring—are represented in North America as well, including *A. muscaria* var. *guessowii*, with an orange or yellow cap; all-white *A. muscaria* var. *alba*; and *A. muscaria* var. *persicina*, which fruits in lovely shades of peach and salmon.

HABITAT & ECOLOGY: Growing from the soil and mycorrhizal with conifers and hardwoods, fruiting alone or in groups, sometimes forming large arcs or fairy rings.

DISTRIBUTION: *A. muscaria* subsp. *flavivolvata*—Pacific Northwest, Rocky Mountains, rarely in the eastern United States; *A. muscaria* var. *guessowii*—eastern United States; *A. muscaria* var. *alba*—northern United States; *A. muscaria* var. *persicina*—eastern United States, predominantly in the South.

SEASON: Summer, fall, and over winter along the California coast.

PHYSICAL DESCRIPTION: Immature fruiting body at first enclosed in a white to light yellow egg-shaped universal veil (volva). Caps of mature mushrooms range from 2" to 10" (5–25 cm) across, nearly spherical at first and flattening with age, retaining cottony veil remnants in the form of raised warts. Closely spaced gills are white to cream and very finely attached or completely free from the stem. The white stem is up to 1¼" (3 cm) wide and up to 8" (20 cm) long, with a high, pendant, skirt-like partial veil remnant. The stem ends in a basal bulb covered in concentric rings of shaggy-textured universal veil remnants. Spore print white.

GILLED POLYPORE

Trametes betulina

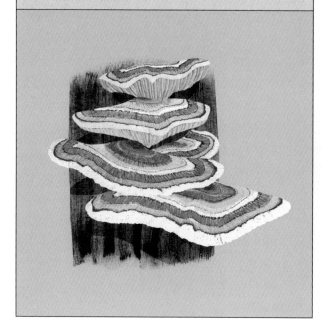

Don't judge a book by its cover, and don't judge a mushroom by its cap. Take, for example, the gilled polypore, the oxymoron of the mushroom world. By definition "polypore" means "many pores," a perfect description of the pockmarked fertile undersurface typical of this group of fungi. The upper surfaces of gilled polypore mushrooms display beautiful, concentric zones of alternating warm colors, and they can easily be mistaken for other similar-looking species such as turkey tails (*Trametes versicolor*). But, as this fungus beautifully demonstrates, it is equally important to look at the underside of a mushroom. Surprisingly, a peek at the bottom reveals that, as the common name suggests, it appears to have gills instead of pores. To add to the enigma, the gills of *T. betulina* are not true gills but are actually large, elongated pores. Their texture is reminiscent of the loveliest brain corals, and their radial arrangement lends them a stunning optical illusion effect.

Whether gills or pores, the unusual morphology of the fertile surface of the gilled polypore serves one purpose—to maximize the spore-producing surface of the mushroom. True gilled mushrooms tend to be soft, fragile, and ephemeral, which limits their lifespan and therefore their window of spore dispersal. Gilled polypores, by contrast, are tough, thick, and leathery—traits that make them durable enough to last an entire season, even through severe weather and drought—an advantage that drastically increases the length of time they are able to release spores. In colder parts of the country, gilled polypore mushrooms are one of a handful of species to persist through winter, often making it to spring in perfect condition despite having been buried in snow and ice for several months.

HABITAT & ECOLOGY: Annual, saprobic, growing singly or in overlapping clusters on decaying hardwood (and very occasionally conifer) branches and logs.

DISTRIBUTION: Widely distributed.

SEASON: Summer and fall, older fruiting bodies often overwintering.

PHYSICAL DESCRIPTION: Semicircular, kidney- or bracket-shaped caps are up to 4" (10 cm) across and 1" (2.5 cm) thick. The lightly fuzzy upper surface is zoned with concentric rings of tan, gray, cream, light yellow, and soft orange. The undersurface is made up of radially arranged, elongated gill-shaped pores. Spore print white.

GREEN ELF CUP

Chlorociboria aeruginascens and *C. aeruginosa*

What teeny, tiny green elf cups lack in size, they make up for with their huge wow factor. One of the prettiest and most unique mushrooms, they produce a brilliant pigment called **xylindein**, giving them an all-over teal-blue color not commonly found in the natural world. As the fungus grows, the mycelium often stains its substrate wood the same bright turquoise color, inspiring the common name "green stain fungus." The unusually colored wood, also known as green oak, is highly prized by woodworkers for use in detailed inlays on items such as decorative boxes. The most famous example of this is Tunbridge ware style, which was popular in England during the eighteenth and nineteenth centuries. Xylindein also shows great promise as a nontoxic, eco-friendly alternative to synthetic dyes used in the textile and clothing industry.

Considered a "holy grail" species, many mushroom hunters have spent years in search of these elusive mushrooms to no avail. Green elf cup fungi fruiting bodies are extremely small—often ¼" (6 mm) or less across—and often grow out of sight on the underside of well-rotted downed branches and logs, two factors that can make them challenging to spot. The best tactic is to keep an eye out for bright blue-green wood lying on the forest floor. The miniature cups can be easily overlooked, but with luck and a keen eye, a close inspection of the underside of the wood may reveal a colony of these striking woodland treasures.

HABITAT & ECOLOGY: Saprobic, often on the undersides of moist, well-rotted, bark-free branches and logs in mixed hardwood and coniferous forests.

DISTRIBUTION: Widely distributed.

SEASON: The blue-stained wood can be found year-round, but the fruiting bodies typically appear in late summer and fall and may occasionally overwinter.

PHYSICAL DESCRIPTION: Teal blue to blue-green cup-shaped fruiting bodies range from less than ¼" (6 mm) to, less commonly, ½" (1.25 cm) across and are attached to their wood substrate by a tiny, sometimes off-center, stem. Upper and lower surfaces are smooth and similarly colored. Though *Chlorociboria aeruginascens* is more common in North America than *C. aeruginosa*, they look practically identical to the naked eye and can be reliably distinguished only by observing their differing spore shapes under a microscope. Spore print white.

HEDGEHOG MUSHROOM

Hydnum Species

Fungi have evolved many ingenious ways of ensuring reproductive success. Adaptations such as the numerous folds of
gilled mushrooms or the pore tubes of boletes increase the
area of their reproductive surfaces, maximizing their ability to produce as many spores as possible. *Hydnum* species

mushrooms belong to a group of fungi that have taken a different approach. From the top they look like most ordinary gilled mushrooms, but the underside of their caps are covered in dense, soft, comblike teeth that hang down like tiny icicles. The many spiny projections, covered in spore-producing tissue, inspire the common names of "hedgehog" or "wood hedgehog."

Also known as "sweet tooth," these mushrooms are a delicious edible. They have a pleasant, fruity scent similar to their cousins, the chanterelles, but their flavor is earthier and nuttier. The texture of their flesh is satisfyingly firm, almost crisp, making them a good choice for people who are turned off by the chewy texture of some mushrooms. Hedgehogs are extremely versatile and can be used in any dish that calls for mushrooms.

Luckily, the distinctive teeth, along with a few other identifying features, make these easy to recognize, even for beginning foragers. One common species in the United States, *Hydnum repandum*, can grow over a long season and get quite large. Sometimes neighboring *H. repandum* mushrooms merge, forming lumpy masses of fused caps. Another common species is *H. umbilicatum*, sometimes known as the "belly button hedgehog" because of the distinctive dimple in the center of the cap. Equally tasty, they are generally smaller in stature and darker in color but have the same telltale toothy underside. Many mushrooms are highly desirable food for woodland creatures including insect larvae and must be harvested young before they become critter hotels. Luckily, hedgehog mushrooms are rarely ever bothered by pests, so even older specimens are usually undamaged, bug-free, and still suitable for eating.

HABITAT & ECOLOGY: Mycorrhizal with both hardwoods and conifers. Growing on the ground among forest duff singly, in groups, or in large arcs or fairy rings. Both species can sometimes be found growing side by side.

DISTRIBUTION: Widely distributed.

SEASON: Midsummer to late fall and over winter into spring in temperate areas.

PHYSICAL DESCRIPTION: The caps of *Hydnum repandum* are creamy or light peach, thick, irregularly lobed, and lumpy, sometimes with several caps fused together. Specimens are generally 2" to 8" (5–20 cm) across, but because they are not prone to pests, a single mushroom can last several months and become much larger. The underside is covered in short, toothy spines that sometimes run partway down the stem. The spines are soft and rub off easily. The thick, off-center stem is typically 1" to 3" (2.5 cm–7.5 cm) long and the same color as the cap. *H. umbilicatum* has the same toothed underside but is generally smaller, at 2" to 3" (5 cm–6.5 cm) across, and a dark peach to light orange color. Compared to *H. repandum*, it has a more uniformly circular cap with a pronounced central indented belly button, and a longer, more slender stem.

HEN OF THE WOODS

Grifola frondosa

Not to be confused with the similarly avian-themed bright orange chicken of the woods, hen of the woods gets its common name from its shaggy, feathery-textured appearance. Tiers and whorls of gray, tan, or brown spoon- or fan-shaped lobes grow from a thick, white base, giving them the appearance of a plump, ruffled bird. The Japanese name, *maitake*, or "dancing mushroom," may have been inspired by its frilly texture—or perhaps by the dances of joyous mushroom hunters upon discovering these highly coveted edible fungi while out foraging.

Though they are widely cultivated, finding hen of the woods in nature is a huge thrill. Besides their status as prized gourmet mushrooms, they can grow to epic proportions. Very large clusters can reach up to 40 inches (100 cm) across and weigh as much as 50 pounds (22 kg) or more. Bigger isn't necessarily better, though, as younger specimens are more tender, while older hens can be tough, harbor insects, and become impregnated with dirt and debris that can be difficult to remove.

Much like farm-raised meat versus wild game, cultivated *maitake* is perfectly palatable, but the taste is much milder than wild hens, whose woodsy flavor is influenced by the complexities of their growing environment. An extremely versatile mushroom, it can be prepared in myriad ways. In addition to being broken into smaller pieces for use in a variety of dishes, hens can be roasted whole, sliced into steaks and grilled, or marinated and made into delectable mushroom jerky.

A type of polypore, hen of the woods are weakly parasitic and grow in large, dense rosettes around the bases and along the shallow roots of their host trees. Their preference is oak, but they will also colonize other hardwoods such as maple. An infected tree can produce many clusters of mushrooms in a season and over many years so, while foragers may be generous with their spoils, they will rarely if ever give away the top-secret locations of their "hen trees."

HABITAT & ECOLOGY: Weakly parasitic at the bases and shallow roots of hardwoods, particularly oak but sometimes maple or other species. May also be saprotrophic on decaying wood. Though found in the forest, they do not require deep shade to thrive so they also frequently pop up in more urban settings such as parks and cemeteries.

DISTRIBUTION: Widely distributed east of the Rocky Mountains.

SEASON: Late summer through fall.

PHYSICAL DESCRIPTION: Tan, grayish-brown, or brown upper surfaces, lower pore surfaces are white and covered in small round pores which run well down the stem. There is an uncommon all-white variation. Whorled tiers of individual cupped or flat fan-shaped lobes arise in stout, dense branches from a thick white base. Each lobe is up to 3" (7.5 cm) across, with whole clumps reaching huge sizes of up to 40" (100 cm) across and weighing as much as 50 lbs. (22 kg) or more, though young clusters of 7 to 15 lbs. (3 kg–7 kg) are more typical and desirable for consumption.

HONEY MUSHROOM

Armillaria Species

When asked to name the largest known living organism, most would say the blue whale at 110 feet long and 200 tons. Surprisingly, the record is in fact held by a fungus—the Humongous Fungus, as it has been nicknamed. In 1998, researchers at the Malheur National Forest in Oregon discovered a honey fungus, *Armillaria solidipes*, whose mycelium is currently estimated to cover 2,385 acres, or nearly four square miles—the equivalent of 1,665 football fields—and it weighs as much as 3,500 tons. Estimated to be as much as 8,650 years old, it is one of the most ancient living things on the planet. Producing visible mushrooms only in autumn, most of the time the fungus is hidden out of sight as a huge, interconnected underground mass of mycelium.

The secret to this fungus's size may lie in a special adaptation developed by some members of the *Armillaria* genus. As parasites, honey mushrooms infect living trees by means of thick, black shoelace-like filaments called **rhizomorphs**. Mycologists have determined that rhizomorphs evolved from mushroom stems. Unlike the typical delicate mycelium of most fungi, these tough rhizomorphs allow a honey fungus to spread for miles, sickening many trees in its path. Once it has infected a tree, the fungus colonizes it from the roots up, eventually girdling it and cutting off its supply of nutrients and water, a process that can take twenty to fifty years. After the tree is dead, the fungus switches roles from parasite to saprobe and continues to feed off the decaying wood. As destructive as this seems, it is part of the natural cycle of a woodland ecosystem. Dead trees provide food and habitats for many species of birds, animals, and insects. The honey fungus, like other decomposers, breaks down the dead wood into nutrients that become available to neighboring forest-dwelling organisms, from the tiniest of microbes to the mightiest of oaks.

There are as many as twelve confirmed honey mushroom species native to the United States, among them *A. solidipes*, simply known as the honey mushroom; the bulbous honey, *A. gallica*; the ringed honey, *A. mellea*; and the ringless honey, *A. tabescens*. In a good year honey mushrooms can fruit in massive numbers, delighting foragers with their bounty, but palatability is a matter of personal taste. Though they are widely consumed, especially in many European countries, they should be parboiled and cooked thoroughly prior to eating, as they can be slightly bitter, a bit slimy, and indigestible to some people. They are not considered a beginner mushroom for inexperienced foragers, as they can be easily confused with poisonous look-alikes, including the deadly toxic funeral bell, *Galerina marginata*.

HABITAT & ECOLOGY: Parasitic and/or saprobic on both conifers and hardwoods. Sprouting from the bases or roots of living trees and decaying logs and stumps, sometimes in staggering numbers. Though they occasionally fruit singly or in small clumps, they can appear in huge clusters of many dozens of mushrooms.

DISTRIBUTION: Widely distributed.

SEASON: Late summer and fall.

PHYSICAL DESCRIPTION: Cap yellow, tan, or brown, sometimes with a scaly texture, especially near the center. Beginning as tight buttons, mature cap size is highly variable, typically ranging from 2" to 5" (3 cm–12 cm), but some specimens can reach the size of a Frisbee. Light-colored gills are closely spaced and either attached to the stem or begin to run down it. Some species have a cottony partial veil covering the mature gills that, after the cap expands, remains high on the stem as a thick membranous or fuzzy ring. Stems are 3" to 8" (7–21 cm) long, bulbous at the base in some species, or tapering to a point and fused together when growing in clumps. Spore print white.

JACK-O'-LANTERN MUSHROOM

Omphalotus Species

The brilliant orange coloring of this mushroom would be reason enough to name it the jack-o'-lantern, but they have a hidden feature that isn't apparent until after the sun goes down. In the dark, these mushrooms emit a faint eerie green glow. Much like other bioluminescent organisms such as algae or fireflies, they produce their own "cold" light by means of chemicals in their gills. One theory, besides being a cool party trick, is that the ghostly light, produced during peak spore production, attracts nocturnal insects that help spread the spores to other areas of the forest.

Jack-o'-lanterns can form impressive colonies, fruiting in sizable groups and with individual caps quite large—up to 10 inches (25 cm) across—a tree or stump covered in tiers of these pumpkin-hued beauties is a sight to behold. These mushrooms are a wood decay species but sometimes appear as though they are growing from the ground. A bit of excavating will often reveal buried roots from a tree that has otherwise been reduced to a stump or may have disappeared completely.

There are two distinct species in the United States, the eastern jack-o'-lantern, *Omphalotus illudens,* and the western jack-o'-lantern, *O. olivascens.* The eastern variety is bright orange from top to bottom. The western variety is tinged with olive green or warm brown tones and can be used to make beautiful violet, gray, or green dyes for yarn and textiles.

Unfortunately, inexperienced foragers sometimes mistake these for edible chanterelles or chicken of the woods.

Though not deadly, all varieties of jack-o'-lanterns contain toxins that cause severe gastrointestinal symptoms that can last for days. There are a number of distinctive features that distinguish them from both chanterelles and chicken of the woods, however, and armed with the proper knowledge, it is easy to avoid confusion between them.

HABITAT & ECOLOGY: Saprobic at the base of stumps and standing trees, infrequently on logs, growing in large clumps of many mushrooms. Sometimes appearing in clusters on lawns from buried decaying roots or stumps of trees that are no longer there.

DISTRIBUTION: Eastern jack-o'-lantern, *Omphalotus illudens* east of the Rocky Mountains; western jack-o'-lantern, *O. olivascens*, California.

SEASON: Fall in the east, fall and winter in the west.

PHYSICAL DESCRIPTION: Caps of eastern jack-o'-lanterns are bright orange; western jack-o'-lanterns are dull orange to olive or brown, especially as they age. Individual caps are button-like at first, becoming flat, then upturned with a wavy edge, and up to 10" (25 cm) across at maturity. The bioluminescent gills are the same color as the cap and run completely down the stem. Stems are 1.5" to 6" (3 cm–15 cm) long by up to 2" (5 cm) thick, tapering toward the base where they attach to the rest of the cluster.

KING BOLETE

Boletus edulis

Boletes are a complex group of mushrooms made up of hundreds of known species worldwide. At one time almost every fleshy-textured mushroom with a cap, stem, and a spongy fertile surface covered in pores—as opposed to gills—was lumped into the genus *Boletus*. Over time these various mushrooms have been reorganized into separate genera based on shared physical characteristics. Modern DNA sequencing continues to cause a seemingly endless shuffling of species, making it difficult to keep up with who's who in the world of boletes.

To make matters more confusing, boletes are notoriously difficult to identify. The differences between them can be subtle, and there are entire books dedicated to trying to tease them apart. Some of the world's most prized edible mushrooms are boletes, but they can have bitter or toxic doppelgängers, so this group of mushrooms is best left to experienced foragers. The exception is the most famous one, *Boletus edulis*. It is known by many names, including cep, porcino, and penny bun in parts of Europe and king bolete in North America. The plump cap looks like a shiny, toasted hamburger bun, and the light-colored, portly stem gives it a distinctive, almost animated appearance that makes it fairly easy to distinguish from poisonous look-alikes. Given enough time, specimens can grow quite large—a 7-pound (3.2 kg) whopper was discovered in Scotland in 1995—but they are most desirable when young and smaller, as they can become soggy insect hotels with age.

Considered one of the most prized culinary mushrooms in the world, it is so revered that many cultures have dishes dedicated entirely to it. Notoriously difficult to cultivate commercially, wild king boletes can be found fresh in summer through autumn months, but they are highly perishable. Luckily, they can be successfully preserved in a number of ways: Dried, canned, and pickled *B. edulis* are distributed and consumed worldwide. They work beautifully in soups, pastas, and risotto, where their complex, nutty flavor and smooth, firm, meaty texture really shine.

HABITAT & ECOLOGY: Found growing from soil singly or in clusters. Mycorrhizal with various species of conifer, occasionally hardwoods.

DISTRIBUTION: Widely distributed, though *Boletus edulis* may actually represent a complex of several closely related species across the United States.

SEASON: Summer and fall.

PHYSICAL DESCRIPTION: The 3" to 12" (7 cm–30 cm) brown, greasy-to tacky-textured caps are dome shaped when young and become broadly convex at maturity. The underside of the cap is covered in a layer of spore-bearing tubes that end in tiny pores which are white and cottony at first, age to greenish yellow, and do not bruise blue. The very stout light-colored stem is club or barrel-shaped and large in proportion to the cap. Typically measuring 3" to 10" (8 cm–25 cm) by up to 4" (10 cm) across at the widest point, the upper portion of the stem is covered in a fine, raised netted texture. In their prime, the flesh is firm, meaty, white all the way through, and does not change color when sliced. They typically weigh in at about 2 pounds (~1 kg) each but can sometimes grow to three times that size. *B. edulis* is sometimes parasitized by *Hypomyces chrysospermus*, the bolete eater fungus.

LION'S MANE

Hericium Species

The lion's mane mushroom, *Hericium erinaceus*, is becoming a household name because of its increasing popularity as a health supplement. Long used in traditional Chinese medicine, the beneficial constituents found in lion's mane are now being studied extensively for their ability to treat or prevent many ailments. Lion's mane has been shown to have anti-inflammatory properties and may prove to be useful in treating inflammation-related maladies such as heart disease, autoimmune disease, and diabetes. It also shows promise in supporting digestive health and immune function, and for treating anxiety and depression. Its biggest claim to fame may be in its benefits to the brain and nervous system: It has been shown to improve mood, focus, and mental clarity and to be a possible treatment or preventative for memory loss and Alzheimer's and Parkinson's diseases. In clinical studies, compounds in lion's mane have been shown to aid in nervous system recovery, including nerve cell repair and regeneration.

Lion's mane is also an excellent culinary mushroom and may be purchased at farmers markets and high-end grocery stores. For those who want to try their hand at fungiculture, it can even be grown at home with widely available countertop grow kits. Luckily for foragers, it is one of three *Hericium* species that grows wild in the United States, all of which are edible. Very distinctive looking and easy to recognize, they belong to a group of mushrooms, known as tooth fungi, that produce their spores on clusters of soft, spiny, pendant projections. *Hericium* can grow from the same tree or log for years, and although they are not uncommon, they can be a bit unpredictable to find. Their mildly sweet flavor and stringy texture are reminiscent of seafood. They're great in stir-fry, chowders, and in just about any recipe calling for fish. Their flavor and texture make for a very convincing version of "crab" cakes.

Hericium means "hedgehog" in Latin and, indeed, their spiky, spiny forms are suggestive of their likewise poky-textured animal namesake. True lion's mane (*H. erinaceus*), also known as old man's beard, forms dense, spherical fruiting bodies that jut out from the sides of trees and logs like large, fuzzy white pom-poms. Bear's head tooth (*H. americanum*) mushrooms look quite similar to lion's mane, but their long spines are arranged more loosely along short, stout branches, giving them a much shaggier, icicle-like appearance. The branches and teeth of coral tooth or comb tooth (*H. coralloides*) are very delicate and finely divided. Its open, airy form resembles frilly lace or frost on a window pane, and small pieces make beautiful garnishes when floated in clear broth soups.

HABITAT & ECOLOGY: Saprobic or parasitic, growing from wounds of dead and occasionally from living trees. Also common on freshly fallen or decaying hardwood logs.

DISTRIBUTION: *Hericium erinaceus* widespread, *H. americanum* east of the Great Plains, *H. coralloides* widely distributed.

SEASON: Summer through fall in cooler climates and late summer into spring in more temperate areas.

PHYSICAL DESCRIPTION: Fruiting bodies are white aging to off-white, yellow, or dingy brown. Lacking a cap, they instead consist of a clump of many long, pointed, pendant, spore-bearing teeth attached to a thick base. *H. erinaceus* is a 2" to 15.5" (5 cm–40 cm) nearly spherical, dense, unbranched mass of pendant teeth up to 2¾" (7 cm) long. *H. americanus* is 6" to 12" (15 cm–30 cm) across, with tight branches covered in rows of pendant teeth up to 2" (5 cm) long. *H. coralloides* is 2" to 10" (5 cm–20 cm) across with loose, delicate coral-like branches covered in clusters and whorls of spiny projections up to ¾" (2 cm) long. Spore print for all species white.

MILK CAP

Lactarius Species

Lactarius is a large genus containing more than five hundred known species worldwide and more than two hundred named species in North America alone. Milk caps, or milky caps, get their common name from the milky "latex" that they exude when cut or damaged. Not actually true latex, this opaque, sticky substance is a defense mechanism to gum up the mouths of hungry critters such as slugs and snails. Some species exude copious amounts of this liquid the instant they are cut, while others barely produce any at all, especially if they are old or growing conditions are dry.

Unlike most mushrooms, which are made up of cylinder-shaped cells, lending them their typical fibrous, stringy texture, the flesh of milk caps is composed of round cells called **sphaerocysts**, which gives them an extremely brittle texture. When bent, the flesh of a milk cap mushroom will snap cleanly like a piece of chalk.

Lactarius identification is notoriously vexing, even to professional mycologists, which has led to the publication of complex keys to aid with this daunting task. Their bleeding milk and brittle flesh make them easy to identify down to the genus, but there are so many varieties, with only subtle differences between some of them, that they can be a real challenge to identify down to species.

The genus *Lactarius* contains members whose edibility ranges from choice to mediocre to poisonous, so when it comes to consumption it's imperative to know the difference. Cap and stem color can help with identification, but so are a host of other features. *Lactarius* are mycorrhizal and, although some are generalists, pairing up with a variety of trees, others will only partner up with specific ones, so it is helpful to note the tree species in the immediate area. The color of the latex—which can be white, cream, yellow, bright orange, or even cobalt blue—is significant, not only when fresh but up to twenty-four hours later. If the milk stains the gills, what color is it? Scent can be key as well (yes, mushroom hunters sniff their mushrooms). And last but not least—this is a trick for experienced foragers only—the taste of the latex, which varies from tasteless, sweet, bitter, peppery, or even burning hot like a chili pepper, can help clinch a final ID.

Several species are commonly eaten in the United States. *Lactarius deliciosus*, the saffron milk cap, has orange latex and bright orange flesh that bruises green. The less common but gorgeous chocolate milky, *L. lignyotus*, is named not for its flavor but for its sumptuous velvety-textured, deep brown cap and stem. Several different species, known as candy caps, have a sweet maple syrup scent and taste that intensifies when dried. They are used as flavoring in desserts, including scrumptious candy cap ice cream.

Arguably the most stunning member of the *Lactarius* genus is the indigo milk cap, *L. indigo*. This substantially sized mushroom, up to 6" (15 cm) across, is true blue from top to bottom and bleeds an intensely brilliant cobalt-colored latex. Its unnatural hue practically screams "don't eat me!" so it may be surprising to know that they're delicious, and when simply fried in a little butter, their firm, crisp texture and unusual coloring adds a nice accent to a variety of dishes.

HABITAT & ECOLOGY: Mycorrhizal with many species of both conifer and hardwood trees, some species being very host specific. Fruiting directly from the ground near their host trees, singly, scattered, in groups, or occasionally large arcs or fairy rings.

DISTRIBUTION: Widely distributed.

SEASON: Year-round depending on the region.

PHYSICAL DESCRIPTION: All species exude milky liquid when cut or damaged. Caps vary from ¾" to 6" (2 cm–15 cm) across and come in many colors, sometimes turning a contrasting color when bruised or as they age. Flat-topped with inrolled edges when young, caps develop a central depression, coming to a shallow funnel shape at maturity. Closely spaced gills run down the stem. Stems are ¾" to 4" (2 cm–10 cm) long and sometimes pitted with "potholes" called **scrobiculi**. Spore print varies.

MOREL

Morchella Species

With its distinctive columnar shape and brown honeycomb-cratered cap, the morel may be one of the most widely recognized mushrooms in the world.

Morels are a highly sought-after gourmet variety, with an earthy, woodsy, nutty flavor and tender texture. Dried morels can demand a high price of $200 or more per pound. Several factors contribute to their expense. Morels have a relatively short growing season, a brief shelf life, and specific growing requirements that most commercial growers have a difficult time replicating, so fresh morels are a bit of a luxury item. Because of this, most morels, even the dried ones in the little bags at the supermarket, are foraged and harvested by hand in the wild, adding to their status and price.

When it comes to foraging these delicacies, it takes a highly trained eye and extensive knowledge of their ecological needs and preferred habitats. Experienced morel hunters work hard, sometimes searching for months or even years to find productive patches, so they guard the whereabouts of their prime foraging spots closely. Some species of morel grow in association with certain kinds of trees, while others grow in wood chips in urban areas, in heavily logged or disturbed areas, or even on burn sites in the wake of forest fires. They all have one thing in common though, and that is that they are extremely difficult to see. Their brown, mottled color blends in with shadows and leaf litter, and their shape is reminiscent of sticks and particularly, pinecones. Though they are highly camouflaged, once you train your eyes to pick out their elusive form, you may find there can be hundreds in one area.

HABITAT & ECOLOGY: Growing alone, scattered, or in large groups in a variety of habitats including in mycorrhizal relationships with specific tree species in forested areas and orchards, in river bottoms, among wood chips and landscaped areas in urban settings, and in locations disturbed by logging and forest fires.

DISTRIBUTION: Various species widely distributed.

SEASON: Spring.

PHYSICAL DESCRIPTION: Cap round, cylindrical, or conical, typically shades of brown, yellowish tan, or grayish brown, sometimes more pointed toward the top, like a Christmas tree. 1¼" to 6" (3 cm–15 cm) tall by 1" to 3" (2 cm–8 cm) across, with deep pits and raised ridges arranged in a honeycomb pattern. Stems are typically white, cream, or tan colored and hollow all the way from the base up through the cap of the mushroom.

OYSTER MUSHROOM

Pleurotus Species

Next to common white buttons, portobellos, and shiitakes, oyster mushrooms are one of the mushrooms most commonly found in American supermarkets. Among the easiest mushrooms to cultivate, even on the kitchen counter thanks to widely available kits, they are grown and consumed worldwide and used extensively in the cuisines of many cultures.

Oyster mushrooms get their common name from their shell-shaped fruiting bodies, not because of how they taste, though some people do say they are slightly reminiscent of seafood. Their delicate flavor is more often described as woodsy with a hint of anise. These versatile mushrooms, with their delectably meaty texture, lend themselves to many types of dishes such as stir-fries and soups, but they are also delicious in a simple sauté with butter, garlic, and a few fresh herbs.

Cultivated oyster mushrooms come in a variety of gorgeous colors. In addition to the white pearl (*Pleurotus ostreatus*), there is a variety that has blue-gray caps that contrast beautifully against their bright white gills. The golden oyster (*P. citrinopileatus*) is bright sunshine yellow, and pink oysters (*P. salmoneo stramineus*) are rich salmon pink.

Luckily for the forager, wild oyster mushrooms are widespread, common, and can fruit in fantastic numbers, particularly after a dramatic shift in weather such as a hot or cool spell followed by rain. Wild varieties are fairly easy to identify, though there are a few inedible or even toxic look-alikes, so it is important to familiarize yourself with the differences. For example, poisonous jack-o'-lantern mushrooms (*Omphalotus* sp.) have a similar shape and habitat but are greenish orange to bright orange, including the gills. Wild oyster mushrooms tend toward white, light gray, or grayish brown with white gills, though the golden oyster has escaped from cultivation and is naturalized in parts of the United States.

Oyster mushrooms are saprobic, but unlike most wood-decomposing fungi, they are also some of the few known carnivorous species, adding meat to their diet as a source of nitrogen. These hunters are stationary, so they produce chemicals that smell like food to attract microscopic worms called **nematodes**. An oyster mushroom's secret weapon is a powerful toxin found on nodules along its mycelium. Hapless victims, lured in by the false prospect of dinner, are paralyzed and then digested from the inside out.

HABITAT & ECOLOGY: Saprobic on deciduous (occasionally coniferous) logs and dead standing trees. Carnivorous as well, preying on microscopic soil nematodes. Fruiting in small clumps or in very large numbers of overlapping shelf-like clusters in open, leafy, mixed deciduous forests.

DISTRIBUTION: Widely distributed.

SEASON: Nearly year-round depending on the species and location.

PHYSICAL DESCRIPTION: Flat, fan, or oyster-shell-shaped fruiting bodies are 1.25" to 10" (3 cm–25 cm) across. Cap surfaces are white, ivory, tan, light gray, or grayish brown. White gills are decurrent (running down) the very short, often off-center stem. The exception is the golden oyster, *Pleurotus citrinopileatus*, which is golden yellow throughout. Spore print white.

SHAGGY MANE INK CAP

Coprinus comatus

"Here one day, gone the next" pretty much sums up the fleeting existence of an ink cap mushroom. Also known as inky caps, this large group of mushrooms gets its name from the unique way in which they release their spores into the environment. In a process of autodigestion called **deliquescence**, ink caps literally turn themselves into liquid. In under twenty-four hours they are reduced to a mere pool of inky black spores. Picking these mushrooms speeds the meltdown, so if they're being harvested for cooking, they need to be used right away or they might end up as a black puddle on the kitchen counter. For those who are feeling crafty, ink cap mushrooms can be used to make actual ink for drawing and writing. As a matter of fact, Merlin Sheldrake used the ink from shaggy mane ink cap mushrooms to illustrate his book *Entangled Life*.

The shaggy mane, shaggy ink cap, or lawyer's wig is one of the most common and widely recognized ink caps. Conspicuous mushrooms, their fairly large, bright white, cylindrical-shaped fruiting bodies have a propensity to pop up in people's lawns, sometimes in large numbers, overnight. The tall, narrow cap of a shaggy mane, with its densely packed gills, traps its spores deep inside where it is impossible for them to make their way out. It solves this dilemma by dissolving itself from the bottom edge up, turning black and curling at the margin to expose its spores to air currents, which carry them to new destinations. Often a group of shaggy manes is in all states at once, with some barely poking their pristine white heads out of the ground, some dripping with gooey black stalactites, and others nothing but a dark smudge in the grass.

Besides being able to radically transform its appearance in a matter of hours, this mushroom has another trick up its sleeve. Ironically, one of the most fragile and temporary of mushrooms can perform daring feats of strength. During growth spurts they are capable of exerting enough upward force to push their way through hard-packed gravel, lift heavy paving stones, and even break apart asphalt.

Young shaggy manes are a tasty edible when still white and firm. They can be consumed after they begin to blacken, but their flavor is diminished and they can turn a dish an unappealing color. Their distinctive appearance makes them fairly easy to identify, they grow in convenient locations, and they can be quite prolific, making them a good choice for novice foragers. This species is known to accumulate environmental toxins in its flesh, so it is important to harvest them from unpolluted areas and from lawns that are free from herbicides, pesticides, and other harmful chemicals.

The common ink cap (*Coprinopsis atramentaria*) is edible as well but comes with a word of caution. Also known as tippler's bane, it contains the compound coprine, which inhibits the body's ability to properly break down alcohol. Interestingly, the prescription medication Antabuse (disulfiram), used for treating alcohol dependence, acts by blocking the same enzymes. Side effects, though not fatal, are extremely unpleasant and can include hot flashes, flushed face, sweating, tingling limbs, vomiting, diarrhea, and in extreme cases, heart palpitations. Coprine poisoning can occur even if alcohol is consumed several days before or after eating.

HABITAT & ECOLOGY: Fruiting singly, in small groups, large troops, or fairy rings in grassy areas such as parks and lawns, gravel driveways and roadsides, and in disturbed areas.

DISTRIBUTION: Widely distributed.

SEASON: Summer through fall.

PHYSICAL DESCRIPTION: Initially egg shaped, becoming columnar and eventually like a deep bell, with a mature size of 2" to 6" (5 cm–15 cm) tall by 2" (6 cm) in diameter. The cap, white with a brown patch at the top and covered in overlapping layers of large, recurved scales, turns black from the bottom edge up as it deliquesces. The entire mushroom eventually melts into black liquid. The gills are initially white but turn black as spores are produced. The white, hollow, extremely brittle stem is an average of ½" (13 mm) in diameter by up to 12" (30 cm) tall. There is a fragile ring of white tissue around the stem that often becomes loose and falls to the base of the mushroom. Spore print is black.

SPLIT GILL

Schizophyllum commune

Split gill mushrooms, also called gillies, are one of the most successful and widespread species of fungus in the world, found practically anywhere there is wood and on every continent except Antarctica.

Part of their success as an organism lies in the fact that

they are rugged. Unlike softer mushrooms whose average lifespan is only a couple of weeks at best—or as little as twenty-four hours in the case of ink caps—the flesh of split gills is tough and leathery. This gives the fruiting bodies longevity, resistance to repeated periods of drought, and even the ability to overwinter in cold climates. A split gill can dry out considerably and lie dormant for long periods of time, but when it rains the densely hairy upper surface of the cap acts like a sponge, rehydrating the mushroom and allowing it to spring back into reproductive action.

A close inspection of the undersurface reveals how this fungus gets its common name. What look like centrally radiating gills at first glance are actually specialized folds—each with a split down the middle—a unique evolutionary adaptation that lends them a long window of spore production. When their environment is sufficiently moist, the folds open, releasing spores into the damp surroundings, where they are most likely to germinate successfully. During dry periods the folds clamp shut, and the mushroom shuts down spore production, hunkering down until the next wet spell, conserving spore production for when the conditions are most ideal.

The most astounding—and difficult to grasp—

reproductive adaptation of *Schizophyllum commune* is that they have as many as twenty-eight thousand different sexes, or distinctive mating types. Unlike the 50 percent success rate of humans, this affords split gill spores a nearly 100 percent chance of reproductive compatibility when bumping into other spores in the woods.

Split gills are not toxic, but because of their dry, leathery texture they're not generally considered a choice edible. However, they are widely consumed in Mexico, parts of the tropics, and India—where they are an ingredient in a type of pancake—because their durability is an advantage over softer mushrooms that perish quickly in the heat.

HABITAT & ECOLOGY: Saprobic, occasionally fruiting singly but most often in large groupings arranged in overlapping, tiled clusters on the underside of dead hardwood logs, sticks, and branches. Often just the leading edges of the caps can be seen until the substrate is turned over. Sometimes parasitic on live but sickly hardwood trees.

DISTRIBUTION: Widely distributed.

SEASON: Spring through fall, often overwintering.

PHYSICAL DESCRIPTION: Fan- or shell-shaped ⅓" to 2" (1 cm–5 cm) caps are off-white, pinkish tan, tan, or light grayish brown, the edges inrolled at first then becoming wavy and, in larger specimens, lightly or deeply lobed. The upper surface is densely hairy, and the fertile surface is made up of longitudinally split gill-like folds that radiate from a central point. Lacking a stem, they can be attached either centrally or laterally to their substrate. Spore print white.

STINKHORN

Various Species

Fantastically freakish and wonderfully weird in their variations, all stinkhorns have one thing in common: their disgusting smell. Well, disgusting in human terms, anyway. But if you're an insect such as a fly or beetle that loves rotting flesh, stumbling upon a stinkhorn will make your day.

Stinkhorns do not spread their spores by means of air currents like many other species of mushrooms—they have devised an ingenious air delivery service instead. Their spores are contained in a dark, sticky, putrid-smelling liquid called **gleba** that attracts carrion-loving insects by the droves. After having a tasty snack, the insects fly away with the stinkhorn's spores on their feet, spreading them to new locations.

While their smell may be enough to trigger anyone's gag reflex, the, um, "anatomically correct" shape of members of the genus *Phallus* may elicit either a gasp or a giggle, depending on the viewer's modesty and maturity level. Many names given to these mushrooms are suggestive of their indecency: *Phallus duplicatus* is commonly known as "the flasher" and *P. impudicus* translates to "shamelessly phallic." Stinkhorns have no sense of modesty when it comes to where they grow, either, unabashedly cropping up in the bark mulch on playgrounds and brazenly popping up in nicely manicured public gardens. Prudish Victorian folk would go out at dawn and smash stinkhorns to bits to avoid the risk of them making a "bad impression" on pure young ladies taking their morning walks.

A stinkhorn emerges from a structure called a universal veil—a gelatinous egg encased in a thin sac. In some species these eggs are considered edible and are referred to as devil's or witch's eggs, conjuring up images of bubbling cauldrons. Keeping in mind what they eventually look and smell like, this culinary experience should probably be reserved for double-dog dares or the gastronomically adventurous. Perhaps an acquired taste, their crunchy texture is often compared to water chestnuts, and their flavor described as reminiscent of old musty radishes. Foragers who are brave enough to try them should be 100 percent sure of their identification because immature *Amanita* species mushrooms, which can be deadly poisonous, are also encased in egglike universal veils. Basket stinkhorns (*P. indusiatus*), with their fabulously lacy, netted white skirts are commercially grown in East Asia, where they are considered a delicacy and come with a hefty price tag. A dried version is available in Asian markets and can be rehydrated for use in soups.

The dog stinkhorn (*Mutinus caninus*) and the devil's dipstick (*M. elegans*) are no less stinky or immodest and sport sunset shades of hot pink, coral, and orange. Rounding out the stinkhorn sideshow are the totally bizarre cage stinkhorn (*Clathrus ruber*), which looks like a pink wiffle ball; the stinky squid (*Pseudocolus fusiformis*), with its crab claws reaching up out of the ground; and the octopus stinkhorn (a.k.a. devil's fingers, *Clathrus archeri*), a delightfully nightmarish tangle of tentacles that looks as though it belongs in an alien horror movie.

HABITAT & ECOLOGY: Saprobic on decaying organic matter. Stinkhorn eggs may be at or just under the soil line. Occasionally growing singly, they more often fruit in groups. Depending on the species they can be found in forests and very commonly pop up in garden mulch, compost piles, or lawns in cultivated and urban areas.

DISTRIBUTION: Widely distributed.

SEASON: Summer through fall, or year-round in warmer climates.

PHYSICAL DESCRIPTION: The immature fruit bodies are at first enclosed in an egg-like structure called a universal veil. Gelatinous in texture and covered in a thin membrane, the universal veil can vary in color depending on the species. Spores are contained in a dark olive green to brown sticky substance called gleba. General size, color, and shape of mature mushrooms vary greatly from species to species.

TURKEY TAIL

Trametes versicolor

Saprobic turkey tails grow in flowery rosettes and cascading, overlapping clusters on decaying hardwood and are one of the most widely distributed and common mushrooms in the world. There is, however, nothing ordinary about their appearance—a log or stump covered in dozens of these beautiful, multicolored fan-shaped mushrooms is a glorious sight to see.

The species name *versicolor* means "variously colored," an apt name for a fungus whose fruiting bodies appear in endlessly gorgeous combinations of brown, cinnamon, gold, gray, white, lilac, and even shades of true blue. In some instances a single cap may display an entire rainbow of colors. The upper surfaces of the thin, semicircular mushrooms are zonate, meaning composed of concentric bands of contrasting hues. The texture of the bands alternates between smooth and finely hairy or velvety. New zones are produced throughout summer and fall, much like growth rings of a tree. Fruiting bodies that survive more than one season may develop harmless colonies of algae on their upper surfaces, lending them a pretty greenish tint.

Like that of other polypore mushrooms, a turkey tail's off-white- to buff-colored fertile undersurface is made up of spore-producing pores. Along with cap color and texture, the very small pore size (three to six or more pores per millimeter) of *Trametes versicolor* is a feature that can help differentiate true turkey tails from other similar-looking mushroom species.

Turkey tail mushrooms have been used medicinally in Asia for thousands of years to treat cancer and boost the body's immune system. In the United States, functional mushrooms are becoming more widely recognized for their potential use as alternatives to allopathic medications for a wide array of maladies. A subject of much study, in 2012 the US Food and Drug Administration approved a clinical trial to gain more scientific data on *T. versicolor* as an adjunctive therapy to support the immune system of patients undergoing conventional cancer treatments such as chemotherapy.

HABITAT & ECOLOGY: Saprobic on decaying hardwood logs, stumps, and branches, growing in dense, cascading tiers along the sides or in rosettes if fruiting along the top. A colony of turkey tails can sometimes cover an entire "nursery" log with hundreds of mushrooms from end to end.

DISTRIBUTION: Widely distributed.

SEASON: Year-round.

PHYSICAL DESCRIPTION: Thin, tough fruit bodies up to 4" (10 cm) across are semicircular, bracket, or rosette shaped, becoming slightly ruffled along the margins. Upper surfaces are patterned with zones of concentric circles in shades of brown, buff, cinnamon, gray, lavender, and even blue. Older specimens are sometimes colonized by harmless algae that can tint the upper surfaces of the caps green. The colorful zones are alternately finely fuzzy and smooth textured. The white-to-cream-colored fertile undersurface is covered in extremely tiny pores. Completely lacking stems, they are laterally attached to their substrate. Spore print whitish.

WOOD BLEWIT

Clitocybe nuda

The purple-hued wood blewit is undoubtedly one of the prettiest fall mushrooms. Wood blewits have a stocky build with a classic cap-and-stem shape, similar in form and stature to the common white button mushrooms found in grocery stores. But when wood blewits are fresh, every part of them, even the gills, are lovely shades of purple ranging from brilliant amethyst to bright violet through soft lilac. They can become trickier to identify as they age because they tend to lose their intense color quickly. The caps fade to shades of tan and buff, but the gills and stem often retain some of their distinctive purple coloring.

Smelling wild mushrooms may seem like a strange thing to do, but scent can be key to identification. While some mushrooms smell like bleach, rotting cabbage, or decaying flesh—odors that are offensive to humans—others have pleasing scents such as anise, apricots, or maraschino cherries. Despite their grape-y purple color, wood blewits have a sweet, earthy scent reminiscent of orange juice concentrate.

Considered a choice edible by some, wood blewits can be compared to white button mushrooms in texture, though their flavor is more distinctively woodsy. Some specimens may be bitter depending on where they are growing and how fresh they are. They should always be cooked thoroughly, as they are indigestible when raw and can still cause gastrointestinal upset in a small percentage of sensitive people even with proper preparation. Wood blewits can be confused with similar-looking inedible or toxic purple mushrooms such as some webcap (*Cortinarius*) species. Webcaps have a **cortina**—a fibrous membrane that protects the mushroom's developing gills—and a rusty brown spore print, whereas wood blewits lack a cortina and have a pink spore print. The differences can be subtle, so gathering wood blewits for food is advisable only for more experienced foragers.

Wood blewits typically act as saprobes, thriving on organic matter such as deep piles of rotting leaves, but under low nutrient conditions they become resourceful hunters. Penetrating neighboring colonies of soil bacteria, they liquify them into an easily absorbed nutritive soup.

HABITAT & ECOLOGY: Saprobic, particularly on thick piles of leaf litter and other decaying organic matter in forest or urban habitats, and even on compost piles. Growing singly, scattered, in groups, or commonly forming large arcs or fairy rings.

DISTRIBUTION: Widely distributed.

SEASON: Late summer and fall, or into winter in milder areas.

PHYSICAL DESCRIPTION: Caps are 1¼" to 6" (3 cm–15 cm) across, lightly domed, with an inrolled margin when immature and become convex to nearly flat with wavy margins as they age. Fresh, young caps are waxy or greasy textured and range from bright purple to violet and light lilac but age to buff or tan with a silky, dry sheen. The closely spaced gills, colored like the cap, often retain their purple coloring and are either attached to the stem or may run down it slightly. The up to 1½" (4 cm) thick stout purple stem often has a swollen base covered in lavender mycelial fuzz and may be embedded with debris such as sticks and leaves.

ASSOCIATIONS, CLUBS, AND CITIZEN SCIENCE RESOURCES

Fungal Diversity Survey, www.fundis.org

iNaturalist, www.inaturalist.org

Mycological Society of America, www.msafungi.org

North American Mycological Association, www.namyco.org

WEBSITES

First Nature, www.first-nature.com/fungi/~id-guide.php

Fungi Growing on Wood (Messiah College), www.messiah.edu/Oakes/
fungi_on_wood/index.htm

Learn Your Land, www.learnyourland.com

Mushroom Expert, www.mushroomexpert.com

Tom Volk's Fungus of the Month, botit.botany.wisc.edu/toms_fungi/fotm.
html

FIELD GUIDES

A general field guide to North American mushrooms is a valuable asset, and
a field guide specific to your area is an indispensable tool. Luckily there are
guides that cover every region of the United States.

North American

Peterson Field Guide To Mushrooms of North America, Second Edition,
Karl B. McKnight, Joseph R. Rohrer, Kirsten McKnight Ward, and Kent
H. McKnight

National Audubon Society Field Guide to North American Mushrooms,
National Audubon Society

Regional

*All That the Rain Promises and More: A Hip Pocket Guide to Western
Mushrooms*, David Arora

Appalachian Mushrooms: A Field Guide, Walter E. Sturgeon

Field Guide to Wild Mushrooms of Pennsylvania and the Mid-Atlantic: Revised and Expanded Edition, Bill Russell

Mushrooms of the Gulf Coast States: A Field Guide to Texas, Louisiana, Mississippi, Alabama, and Florida, Alan E. Bessette, Arleen R. Bessette, and David P. Lewis

Mushrooms of the Midwest, Michael Kuo and Andrew S. Methven

Mushrooms of the Northeast: A Simple Guide to Common Mushrooms, Teresa Marrone and Walt Sturgeon

Mushrooms of the Northwest: A Simple Guide to Common Mushrooms, Teresa Marrone and Drew Parker

Mushrooms of the Redwood Coast: A Comprehensive Guide to the Fungi of Coastal Northern California, Noah Siegel and Christian Schwarz

Mushrooms of the Rocky Mountain Region, Vera Stucky Evenson and Denver Botanic Gardens

Mushrooms of the Southeast, Todd F. Elliott and Steven L. Stephenson

Mushrooms of the Upper Midwest: A Simple Guide to Common Mushrooms, Teresa Marrone and Kathy Yerich

ECOLOGY & FORAGING

Entangled Life, Merlin Sheldrake

Finding the Mother Tree: Discovering the Wisdom of the Forest, Suzanne Simard

The Future is Fungi: How Fungi Can Feed Us, Heal Us, Free Us and Save Our World, Michael Lim and Yun Shu

Growing Gourmet and Medicinal Mushrooms, Paul Stamets

How to Forage for Mushrooms without Dying: An Absolute Beginner's Guide to Identifying 29 Wild, Edible Mushrooms, Frank Hyman

Mycelium Running: How Mushrooms Can Help Save the World, Paul Stamets

Mycophilia: Revelations from the Weird World of Mushrooms, Eugenia Bone

About the Author

O n most days, mycologist, educator, and nature photographer **Meg Madden** can be found in the forests of her childhood practicing what she calls "mushroom yoga": lying on the ground, standing on her head, balancing precariously on a log, or in any number of awkward positions to capture the perfect snail's-eye view of her favorite photo subject—fungi! Her colorful, highly detailed mushroom portraits offer an intimate look into the often-overlooked world of these extraordinary organisms. Inspired by the belief that people are more likely to take care of something they love, Meg finds great joy in facilitating fun and meaningful connections between humans and nature. Meg shares her knowledge and contagious passion for the fantastic world of fungi through visually engaging presentations, mushroom walks, community science projects, and via her Instagram gallery @megmaddendesign.